COWGIRLS

Conceived By
MARY MURFITT

Book By
BETSY HOWIE

Music and Lyrics By
MARY MURFITT

★

★

DRAMATISTS
PLAY SERVICE
INC.

COWGIRLS was produced by Denise Cooper, Susan Gallin, Rodger Hess and Suki Sandler at the Minetta Lane Theatre, in New York City, in April, 1996. It was directed and choreographed by Eleanor Reissa; the set design was by James Noone; the costume design was by Catherine Zuber; the lighting design was by Kenneth Posner; the sound design was by Scott Stauffer; the musical arrangements were by Mary Ehlinger; the musical direction was by Pam Drews Phillips; and the production stage manager was William Joseph Barnes. The cast was as follows:

JO CARLSON .... Rhonda Coullet

RITA .... Mary Ehlinger

LEE .... Lori Fischer

MARY LOU .... Mary Murfitt

MO .... Betsy Howie

MICKEY .... Jackie Sanders

COWGIRLS was produced by the Old Globe Theatre, in San Diego, California, on January 13, 1996. It was directed and choreographed by Eleanor Reissa; the set design was by James Noone; the costume design was by Catherine Zuber; the lighting design was by Kenneth Posner; the sound design was by Jeff Ladman; the musical arrangements were by Mary Ehlinger; and the stage manager was Peter Van Dyke. The cast was as follows:

JO CARLSON. .... Rhonda Coullet

RITA .... Mary Ehlinger

LEE .... Lori Fischer

MARY LOU .... Mary Murfitt

MO .... Betsy Howie

MICKEY .... Jackie Sanders

CHARACTERS

JO CARLSON — Late 40s. Owner of Hiram Hall. If fate hadn't intervened she would have been the next Loretta Lynn/Dolly Parton. As it is, she is the forceful owner of a Music Hall that has seen its better day. She is potentially at the beginning of a brand new chapter in her life with the recent death of her father and subsequent inheritance of Hiram Hall. Jo plays piano and guitar.

MARY LOU — Mid 30s. Violinist/Mandolin. She is the most repressed, inflexible member of the trio. She's been following rules for so long that she no longer knows the difference between what she wants to do and what she should do. Although she doesn't realize it, her subconscious is trying to tell her it's time to do what she wants. Mary Lou plays violin (fiddle), mandolin, and guitar.

RITA — Mid 30s. Pianist. The well-meaning, if somewhat confused, organizer of the summer tour of the Coghill Trio. Her role as wife and mother-to-be has a great deal to do with her confusion. She is seven months into a nine month deadline to figure out what she's going to do with the rest of her life. Rita plays piano, synthesizer, accordian, harmonica, and bucket.

LEE — Mid 30s. Cellist/Guitar. A great explorer of the spiritual frontier, she's always looking for the order in the chaos. She is never without a personal mission and that is particularly true right now. All of this, however, does not preclude a good sense of humor. Lee plays cello, guitar, and tambourine.

MICKEY — Late 20s. The "rode hard and put away wet" waitress at Hiram Hall. She's younger and more spirited than she ought to be for the amount of life she's lived. She doesn't appear to be Nashville's next sweetheart but that won't stop her. Mickey plays banjo and tambourine.

MO — 20s. She's got a special knack for numbers, cooking, and finding the question in what everybody else thought was an answer. Sincere and big-hearted, she is Mickey's greatest fan and Jo's most loyal employee. Mo plays autoharp, ukulele, and bucket.

SETTING

Hiram Hall, a country western saloon in Rexford, Kansas. Time is the present. The first act takes place on a Friday. The second act takes place on Saturday.

INTERMISSION NOTE: House music should actually originate from the jukebox on stage.

MUSICAL NUMBERS

Music and lyrics by Mary Murfitt (with assistance from J. Brahms, F. Chopin, F. Kreisler, and W. A. Mozart).

ACT ONE

1. THE OVERTURE:
    BEETHOVEN SONATA PATHETIQUE, OPUS 13
    (The Trio: Rita, Lee, Mary Lou)

2. THREE LITTLE MAIDS
    Gilbert and Sullivan
    (The Trio)

3. JESSE'S LULLABY
    (Rita with Lee, Mary Lou)

4. ODE TO CONNIE CARLSON
    (Mickey, Mo)

5. SIGMA, ALPHA, IOTA
    (Rita, Lee, Mary Lou)

6. ODE TO JO
    (Mickey, Mo)

7. FROM CHOPIN TO COUNTRY
    (Rita, Lee, Mary Lou)

8. KINGDOM OF COUNTRY
    (Jo, Trio)

9. SONGS MY MAMA SANG
    (Jo, Mary Lou)

10. HEADS OR TAILS
    (Lee, Rita)

11. LOVE'S SORROW
    (Jo, Rita, Lee)

12. LOOKING FOR A MIRACLE
    (Mary Lou, Jo and Company)

ACT TWO

1. DON'T CALL ME TRAILER TRASH
    (Mickey, Mo)

2. HONKY TONK GIRL
    (Rita)

3. EVERY SATURDAY NIGHT
    (Jo, Trio)

4. DON'T LOOK DOWN
    (Lee with Rita)

5. THEY'RE ALL COWGIRLS TO ME
    (Jo, Trio)

6. SADDLE TRAMP BLUES
    (Mary Lou with Rita, Lee)

7. IT'S TIME TO COME HOME
    (Jo)

8. WE'RE A TRAVELIN' TRIO
    (The Trio)

9. SUNFLOWER
    (The Trio)

10. CONCERT MEDLEY
    (Company)

11. HOUSE RULES
    (Jo and Company)

12. COWGIRLS
    (The Trio)

COWGIRLS

ACT ONE

The set is an old country-western bar. The fixtures and furnishings look like they haven't changed since it was built. A staircase leads up to Jo's office that looks over the space. Everywhere there are signs of a face-lift; tarps, ladders, buckets and brooms.

Pre-show music is heard from the jukebox: Hank Williams, Conway Twitty, Porter Wagoner.* The preset fades to black as the music continues. In blackness, the country music ends. A light comes up on Jo's office. She is on the phone.

JO.   Clean up's coming along, Ralph. Gonna be a hellava Grand Reopening thanks to you and the bank! I found me the greatest all-girl, country-western band! Wait'll you hear 'em! Ralph, I'm bettin' they blow the roof off the place! *(The first chord of Beethoven's Sonata* is heard. Lights up on Rita, Lee and Mary Lou, The Trio. [See score for specific cueing of the following speeches.])*

Oh! About that touch-up loan …

I know …

I know …

I know I owe you a lot but you never said no to my daddy in 35 years!

Papers?

What papers?!

(Mo enters. She is stopped by the music and immediately exits. She reenters with Mickey.)

MICKEY.   JO! JO!

JO.

Fax machine? No, I ain't got no fax machine!

I'm across the street!! I'm comin' over!

(She hangs up the phone and exits her office. She is met with the dramatic conclusion of the Sonata. Within the conclusion:)

What the hell?

(The Sonata ends.)

* See Special Note on Songs and Recordings on copyright page.

Real pretty, girls, but I think you're lookin' for the St. Cecelia's Musi-cal Soci-ety. Mickey!

MICKEY.   You ready to hear my song for tomorrow night, Jo?

RITA.   Excuse me?

JO.   I said it was a fine joke. I don't know who put you up to it but you had me goin' for a minute there. Now if you don't mind, I gotta a new band com-ing in — I don't have time to chat. *(To Mickey and Mo.)* Where in the hell's my Cowgirl Trio?

MICKEY.   No sign, Jo ... I thought you were gonna give us a chance ...

JO.   I told you before, Mickey, I ain't puttin' you gals on stage opening night.

RITA.   Excuse me, ma'am, but we're looking for Jo Carlson?

JO.   Yeah? Well, that's me.

RITA.   Wonderful. It's a pleasure to meet you.

JO.   Thank you.... And who the hell are you?

RITA.   We're your trio.

JO.   You're my what?

MICKEY.   You're her what?

MO.   You're her what?

LEE.   Trio. We're the trio.

JO.   You're The Cowgirl Trio?

LEE.   Cowgirl Trio? No. Coghill Trio. We're the Coghill Trio.

JO.   Coghill?

RITA.   Cowgirl???!! Cow ... girl???!! Cog-hill ... cog-hill ... cog-hill ... cowgill ... coggirl ... coghill —

MARY LOU.   This is another illegitimate engagement, isn't Rita? We are about to officially close our infamous reunion tour without ever once having played in the right place, at the right time, to the right people. That's what happen-ing, isn't it, Rita? RITA!!!

LEE.   Listen, Ms. Carlson — there seems to be a mix-up ...

MICKEY.   I'll say. *(Rita takes out a brochure from her briefcase.)*

RITA.   This is Hiram Hall?

JO.   Yes.

RITA.   And we're in Rexford, Kansas ... *(Checking her brochure.)* The sunflower state and home of the world's largest ball of twine?

JO.   Yes.

RITA.   Well, then this is the place! Absolutely. You remember. We spoke on the phone, I said "Hello, my name is Rita, I'm with the Cog-hill Trio." Then you said —

JO.   Yeah, well, whatever got said — this ain't gonna work out.

RITA.   Nooo. Don't say that.

JO.   Look, you ain't country and you ain't singers!!

MARY LOU.   Now that's enough! Certainly we can sing. Girls! Women? *(She hums a pitch. They follow her lead into "THREE LITTLE MAIDS FROM SCHOOL.")*

RITA, LEE and MARY LOU.

> THREE LITTLE MAIDS FROM SCHOOL ARE WE.
>
> PERT AS A SCHOOL GIRL WELL SHOULD BE,
>
> FILLED TO THE BRIM WITH GIRLISH GLEE.
>
> THREE LITTLE MAIDS FROM SCHOOL,
>
> THREE LITTLE MAIDS FROM SCHOOL.

JO.   Listen, ladies, I'm sorry you came all this way but I gotta get on the horn and get myself a new act!

MICKEY.   Hey, Jo...?

JO.   I told ya, Mickey ... the answer's no ... *(To the women.)* What the hell's a coghill anyway?

MARY LOU.   We are alumni of Coghill College, Ms. Carlson.

JO.   I see.

RITA.   I don't want you to think I meant to mislead you.

JO.   Best a luck to you gals.

LEE.   Give us a chance — we play gigs like this all the time.

JO.   Don't forget to stop by the Great Ball O' Twine 'fore you head out. Mickey! Get on over to the bank. Ralph Bell has some damn papers I'm supposed to see. *(Mickey goes for the door. Mo starts to follow.)* And come right back!! Mo —

MO.   I'll stay here.

JO.   You stay here. *(Jo exits.)*

MICKEY.   Happy Trails! *(She exits. Mo continues her work.)*

MARY LOU.   Gigs?! Gigs??!!

LEE.   Gigs. Concerts. It's all music. We can do this. We're very versatile.

MARY LOU.   Yes. We can come and we can go.

LEE.   Mary Lou, I suggest you open your mind to this. You are the one who insisted we continue this tour.

MARY LOU.   That was before Peoria. *(Mo exits.)*

LEE.   I refuse to give up so easily …

MARY LOU.   Easily!! Shall I review it for you? We arrived in Dubuque on June 7 instead of July 6. We were overshadowed by the Bingo caller in Omaha. The audience forgot to arrive in Skokie. Easily?!! The whole tour is a complete wash-out.

RITA.   And it's all my fault!!!???

LEE.   You know, this place is kind of avant garde.

MARY LOU.   Who ever heard of Hiram Hall?

RITA.   I don't know. I was thinking Carnegie Hall, Avery Fisher Hall — Hiram Hall —

MARY LOU.   Where are we playing next, Rita? Monty Hall?

RITA.   You don't have to be so mean, Mary Lou!!

MARY LOU.   Well look where we are!!

RITA.   It was an honest mistake!! I'm trying to balance a lot of different things right now. I can't do it all!! *(She jumps a little and puts a hand on her belly.)*

LEE.   Are you all right?

RITA.   I think the baby's upset with me too — *(Lee puts a hand on the piano to plunk out "Brahm's Lullaby."*)*

LEE.

LA-LA-LA … GO TO SLEEP LITTLE — ?

RITA.   Jesse —

LEE.

JESSE — CLOSE YOUR EYES AND START TO YAWN,

PLEASANT DREAMS UNTIL THE DAWN.

RITA.   It's working. *(Rita takes over the playing. She segues into "JESSE'S LULLABY."*)*

JESSE MY SWEET, YOUR MAMMA'S SO CRAZY —

WELL, THAT'S THE OPINION OF YOUR GRANDMA AND DAD.

* See Special Note on Songs and Recordings on copyright page.

JESSE MY LOVE, DO I REALLY DESERVE YOU?

ALL I SEEM TO DO IS MAKE PEOPLE MAD.

LEE.

JESSE — YOUR MOTHER, THERE ISN'T ANOTHER

WHO'S AS FUNNY AND LOVING AS SHE.

MARY LOU.

JESSE, HOW ARE YOU? THIS IS AUNT MARY LOU.

YOUR MOTHER'S AS TALENTED AS ME.

YOU'LL BE A VIOLINIST.

RITA.

WILL YOU LOOK JUST LIKE ME?

MARY LOU.

YOU'LL BE A CONDUCTOR.

LEE.

YOU'LL BE WHAT YOU'LL BE ...

RITA.

I'LL LOVE YOU WITH ALL MY HEART.

LEE.

I'VE ALREADY DONE YOUR CHART.

RITA, LEE and MARY LOU.

WE CAN'T WAIT 'TIL WE MEET YOU.

RITA.

PLEASE DON'T COME BEFORE YOU'RE DUE.

(Mary Lou, choked up, dabs her eyes, blows her nose.)

MARY LOU.   Allergies. *(Mickey enters with an envelope. Mo enters.)*

MICKEY.   What are y'all still doin' here? Jo told you to clear out.... You're not gonna open up tomorrow night.

LEE.   That remains to be seen.

MICKEY.   I don't think so ... in fact, Jo said we should help you pack.

MO.   She did? I didn't hear that.

LEE.   Hi, I'm Lee, this is Rita and that's Mary Lou.

MICKEY.   I don't care what your names are ... I ain't gonna be usin' 'em.

MO.   What are you going to call 'em then? *(Mo introduces herself to each of them.)* I'm Mo ... I'm Mo ... Mo.

MICKEY.   Ain't so easy, you know. Ain't like you're playin' some two-bit honky tonk. This here is Hiram Hall!

LEE.   Give us a break, Mickey. What's the big deal here?

MICKEY.   What's the big deal here? What's the big deal here?! Hiram Hall was THE hottest music hall this state ever saw.

MARY LOU.   Is it presumptuous to assume that that no longer is the case?

MICKEY.   I don't know but it ain't true anymore, I'll tell you that much.

RITA.   What happened?

MO.   It was a dark and stormy night ...

MICKEY.   Mo! Look, ya'll 'sposed to be clearin' out.

LEE.   Come on, Mickey.

MO.   Hey, Mickey — you could sing 'em your song.... As it happens, Mickey wrote a song about it.

MICKEY.   I don't think so—

MO.   Come on, Mic — you sing it every day.

MICKEY.   Not now —

MO.   Mickey!

MICKEY.   Nah.

MO.   OK. Never mind.

MICKEY.   Well, I suppose I could.

MO.   *(To the trio.)* Sit down! *(Mo gets her autoharp.)* It's a little tune she calls "Ode to Connie Carlson."

MICKEY.   *(To Mo.)* How's my hair? *(Mo gives her a thumbs up.)* Hit it, Mo! *(Mo strums the autoharp as Mickey begins "THE BALLAD OF CONNIE CARLSON.")*

> CONNIE CARLSON WAS THE GREATEST SINGER THIS PLACE EVER SAW

> BUT ONE DARK AND STORMY NIGHT, SHE TOOK OFF AND LEFT JO'S PA.

> WHEN JO WAS FIVE HER DADDY SAID HER MA COULD SING NO MORE

'CAUSE NOW SHE WAS A MOTHER AND THAT'S WHAT GIRLS ARE FOR.

CONNIE HAD HER REASONS, YOU'D DO THE SAME THING TOO,

THE OLD MAN CLIPPED HER WINGS,

SHE COULDN'T FLY, WHAT COULD SHE DO?

SHE PACKED —

(Mo hits a wrong note, then two more, then:)

TRIO. C Major. *(Mo corrects herself and the song continues.)*

MICKEY.

SHE PACKED HER BAGS, KISSED JO GOOD-BYE AND RAN OFF WITH A BAND.

SHE NEVER SHOWED HER FACE AGAIN — BANISHED FROM THIS LAND.

MO. Gone. Evaporated.

MICKEY.

FROM THAT DAY ON JO'S DADDY SAID NO WOMAN COULD SING HERE.

THE PAINFUL MEMORY OF JO'S MA WAS MORE THAN HE COULD BEAR.

HE WIPED OUT EVERY TRACE OF CONNIE IN A JEALOUS RAGE

AND EVEN JO WAS KEPT FROM SINGIN' ON THIS VERY STAGE.

LEE. Jo sings?

MO. Does Jo sing?!

RITA. So whatever happened to Connie Carlson?

MO. Quiet! That part's comin'.

MICKEY.

SOME SAY CONNIE CHANGED HER NAME TO LOUISIANA LOU

BUT THERE'S ALREADY ONE OF HER, SHE SANG WITH SUNSHINE SUE.

OTHERS THINK SHE MET HER TRAGIC END ON A ROAD IN TENNESSEE —

HIT BY A DRUNKEN TRUCKER —

MO.

    WITH A BANJO ON HIS KNEE

    B-A-N-J-O, B-A-N-J-O, B-A-N-J-O —

MARY LOU.   And that's enough for me!

MO.   Good song, huh?

RITA.   So how come he's letting women back on stage now?

MICKEY.   *HE* ain't. Jo is! Her daddy died.

LEE.   How long ago did her mother disappear?

MICKEY.   1959. That was —

MO.   39.

MICKEY.   39 years ago — so the lady that *does* take the stage tomorrow night has to be really good. And don't you worry — Jo knows that — she's gonna get a *great* singer for the Grand Reopenin'.

MO.   Tell 'em about the money part, Mickey.

MICKEY.   Mo!

MO.   I think you should tell them.

MICKEY.   Well, she's pretty close to broke. In fact, if we don't get some money in this place — Jo's headin' straight into the jaws of poverty and misfortune. Which reminds me, I don't have time to be jawin' with ya'll. Come on, Mo.

MO.   It's steamin' time!

MICKEY.   Mo!

MO.   What? We're not steamin' it open this time? We always steam it open, Mickey! *(They exit.)*

MARY LOU.   I'll be in Boston, if you need me.

LEE.   Don't you dare —

RITA.   What are we doing? We can't play country! Can we?

LEE.   Don't be afraid. This place is filled with white light. It's got a great aura.

MARY LOU.   You cannot possibly be suggesting that this is some mystic journey and it all boils down to karma!! I'm sorry — it's simply bad management!! Need I remind you? I gave up a European tour with the La Petit Symphonette! I could have been in Heidelberg. I could have been in Liechtenstein!! I could have been in D sseldorf!!

LEE.   I'm saying we are 3 months into a 3 month tour and finally, as of today, thank God! ... Mercury is no longer in retrograde.

RITA.   Oh, what a relief.

MARY LOU.   I am a classical violinist, Lee! I've had a neck bruise since I was three! I have not sacrificed my entire life to become ... Patsy ... Parton!

LEE.   We have all sacrificed, Mary Lou!

RITA.   Right. I left my husband at home with all my piano students.

MARY LOU.   *(To Lee.)* What about you? What have you sacrificed? You make good money playing questionable music. You have your perfect girlfriend —

LEE.   *Had* my perfect girlfriend. I will never again date someone who has not been analyzed.

RITA.   She's like the sixth one this year, Lee ...

LEE.   It's not easy being a spiritual warrior.

MARY LOU.   What?

LEE.   And by the way, Mary Lou, I *have* sacrificed! I gave up a four disc deal for subliminal realignment recordings in order to do this tour.

MARY LOU.   Subliminal realignment?

RITA.   What is that? I've never understood that.

MARY LOU.   Does it matter?!

LEE.   You might call it "pain-free enlightenment." It's a questioning — "Can we utilize the subconscious mind to fight the negative forces which constantly bombard us and which eventually give rise to chronic back problems?"

MARY LOU.   Oh, who the hell cares?!

RITA.   I'll call Bob — he'll help us —

MARY LOU.   If he's home. Well, he's never home.

RITA.   Oh, Bob told me this wasn't a good idea with the baby and everything but I told him I could handle it. I told him it was my last chance to play with you guys before — before —

LEE.   Come on, Rita ... it's OK. We *all* wanted to play together again. Sure, the universe has thrown us a couple of curve balls ... but I'm glad we did it, aren't you, Mary Lou?

MARY LOU.   Oh, yes. I'm very glad. I'm about to perform in a *bar*.

LEE.   *(To Mary Lou.)* YOU have a very bad attitude.

MARY LOU.   I can't play this stuff!

LEE.   You belong to Sigma Alpha Iota — the finest sorority of female musicians anywhere in the world! And you're going to stand there and tell me you can't play hillbilly music!? It is the same three chords, over and over and over.

MARY LOU.   I can't ... I won't ... I shouldn't play this music.

LEE.   Our finest composers based their greatest works on the folk music of their day ... Beethoven, Dvořák, Copland!

MARY LOU.   We are not Beethoven.

RITA.   I think we should leave before that woman comes back. *(An afterthought.)* Was her hair real?

LEE.   We're not going anywhere.

    SIGMA, ALPHA AND IOTA SISTERS ALL IN MUSIC WE.

MARY LOU.	RITA.
You can't sing that here! No!	Don't do that!!

LEE.

    THOSE BEFORE US SING IN CHORUS WHEN WE PLEDGE OUR
        LOYALTY.

    THOUGH THE ROAD FOREVER WINDING,

    MUSIC'S TIES FOREVER BINDING.

    SUFFRAGETTES THROUGH HISTORY,

    WE WILL BE FOREVER FREE.

(Vocal instrumental.)

    SIGMA, ALPHA AND IOTA, SACRED ARE THE OATHS WE SPOKE.

    HAIL TO THEE, OH MUSE EUTERPE!

    BONDS WE'VE FORGED CAN NE'ER BE BROKE.

    BOUND BY SPIRIT, BOUND BY GENDER

    MUSIC IS OUR GREAT DEFENDER.

    S.A.I. DEAR SISTERS ALL,

    BLESS US HERE IN —

    HIRAM HALL.

MARY LOU.   Oh my God!

RITA.   That really wasn't fair!

MARY LOU.   Lee!! You took a solemn vow of secrecy to never divulge that song!! What if somebody heard us?! What if someone was listening?? How could you?! You can live on the edge if you want to but don't drag us to the precipice!!

LEE.   Sit down, open your chakras, and let's get started.

RITA.   I feel violated.

MARY LOU.   That was extremely manipulative! … So — which one of the three chords should we start with?

LEE.   Maybe we should begin with something we know and try to segue into country.

RITA.   How 'bout Chopin? *(Rita starts playing Nocturne, Opus. No. 5.)*

MARY LOU.   Chopin?!

RITA.   What about words?

LEE.   We'll channel them.

MARY LOU.   Chopin???!!! I don't have this … I don't have music for this!

LEE.

FROM CHOPIN TO COUNTRY IN ONE SINGLE DAY.

RITA.

FROM CHOPIN TO COUNTRY THIS TICKET'S ONE WAY.

LEE.

FROM BRANDENBURG,

RITA.   *(Laughing.)*

TO BRANDIN' COWS.

MARY LOU.   *(Exasperated.)* I could have been in Heidelberg right now!

RITA.   Good, Mary Lou!

LEE.   You made a rhyme!

RITA.   Play the melody. *(They begin to play. Mickey and Mo, with coffee cup, enter.)*

MO.   *(Hushed.)* We just read a top secret, very confidential letter from Ralph Bell at the bank.

MICKEY.   Mo?

MO.   Do you want to know what it said?!

MICKEY.   Mo! This is private!

MO.   That's why I'm talking like this.

MICKEY.   All right, look, I'll tell ya but only so you know how important to-morrow night is … but you don't tell nobody … or I'll be singing your little S.A.I. song from the top of the great ball o' twine!

MARY LOU.   You wouldn't!

MICKEY. From the VERY top — up by the knot.

LEE. What are you talking about?

MICKEY. She owes money that her *Daddy* borrowed.

LEE. How much money?

MICKEY. It's weekly payments of —

MO. 374.67

MICKEY. Right. 67. And she's behind by —

MO. 5 months with interest.

MICKEY. Right. The interest. And it totals out at —

MO. $7493.21!

MICKEY. Right. Seven-hundred-four-thousand-ninety-three dollars —

MO. and 21 cents.

MICKEY. Right! And if she misses one payment the bank's closin' down Hiram Hall forever and turnin' it into a gift shop for the Great Ball 'O Twine.

MARY LOU. It keeps getting worse and worse.

MICKEY. You just clear yourselves out of here. We'll take care of it.

LEE. Mickey, she said you weren't playing either.

MICKEY. No, she didn't.

MO. Yeah, she did, Mickey.

MICKEY. Just clear out!

LEE. Excuse me.

MICKEY. What?!

LEE. What was her name again?

MICKEY. Who?!

LEE. Jo's mother?

MICKEY. Connie Carlson. Why?

LEE. Just curious.

MICKEY. Out! *(Mickey and Mo enter Jo's office.)* Hey, Jo.

MO. Hi, Jo.

JO. Mo, get me a cup —

MO. Cup of coffee. Just the way you like it.

JO.   Thanks, Mo.

MICKEY.   We just wanted to check in on you, see how things are goin'.

MO.   We know it's been a tough time for ya, Jo —

JO.   Did you get the papers from the bank?

MICKEY.   Papers? Oh, yeah, the papers.

MO.   But before you read them papers we thought you might like to hear a little song we wrote for ya. Kind of a pick-me-up onnaconna we think so much of ya, Jo.

JO.   I appreciate the thought girls but I really do need to see the papers —

MICKEY.   Boy, you look nice today, Jo. I like her hair that way. Don't you, Mo?

MO.   Oh, very much.

JO.   The papers?

MICKEY.   Hit it, Mo!

MICKEY and MO.

   ODE TO JO, WE'LL NEVER LEAVE YOUR SIDE.

   OLD RALPH BELL CAN GO TO HELL, BUT US TWO WILL ABIDE.

MICKEY.

   YOU'VE BEEN LIKE A MOTHER TO ME,

MO.

   YOU EAT MY CHILI,

MICKEY.

   AND YOU LIKE MY HAIR.

MICKEY and MO.

   WE'VE BEEN THROUGH A LOT TOGETHER,

   THROUGH ALL KINDS OF STORMY WEATHER,

   JUST GIVE US A CALL AND WE'LL BE THERE.

MO.

   YOU LET ME KEEP MY RABBITS OUT BACK BEHIND THE BAR.

   OTHERS WOULD HAVE COOKED THEM, BUT THAT'S HOW NICE
      YOU ARE.

MICKEY and MO.

JO, WE LOVE YOU. WE'LL ALWAYS BE TRUE BLUE.

SO PLEASE DON'T THINK WE'RE SUCKIN' UP JUST BECAUSE WE WORK FOR YOU.

(Instrumental.)

MICKEY.

YOU'RE GOOD TO ALL MY CHILDREN, YOU'RE ALWAYS FAIR AND WISE.

YOU NEVER TOLD MY HUSBAND I WAS SEEIN' OTHER GUYS.

MICKEY and MO.

JO, WE LOVE YOU, WE'LL ALWAYS BE TRUE BLUE

BUT PLEASE DON'T THINK WE'RE SUCKIN' UP JUST BECAUSE WE WORK FOR YOU.

PLEASE DON'T THINK WE MADE THIS UP JUST BECAUSE WE WORK FOR YOU.

JO.   Thanks, ladies, I've never heard anything quite like it. Now please give me the papers. *(They hand her the paper.)* That son of a bitch!

MICKEY.   Listen Jo, we gotta stick together on this! You know me and Mo here will do whatever we got to!

MO.   Whatever we got to, Jo.

JO.   This is thousands of dollars, ladies, how do you plan to come up with that? And collateral! The man wants collateral?

MICKEY.   OK, then we gotta get us some of that collateral stuff.

JO.   He knows this place is all I got! This ain't even my debt! Daddy used up every last inch of credit this place is ever gonna get!

MICKEY.   You can't give up, Jo. You come too far to let some fat, ugly banker stop ya!

JO.   Sometimes you sound just like your mama, Mickey. Lord, do I miss her right now. She'd figure a way outta this.

MICKEY.   She'da said the same thing about you, Jo.

JO.   What the hell is it about mamas?

MICKEY.   They leave a big hole when they go.

JO.   Damn! I just wanted it to be great. Tomorrow night was gonna prove Daddy wrong — not lettin' Mama sing — not lettin' the ladies sing all those years ...

MICKEY.   You and me could sing together tomorrow night.

JO.   I need you out on the floor, Mickey.

MICKEY.   I could do both.

JO.   It don't work that way, Mickey. I'm not singin' tomorrow night and neither are you. We got enough troubles without you gettin' your heart broke out there in the spotlight.

MO.   Jo? It just occurred to me that we only gotta run at 67% capacity because 139 people paying $7.50 each and drinking two $1.63 beers is equal to or greater than two payments.

JO.   Are you sure, Mo?

MO.   Yeah. Plus those ladies downstairs are booked through the weekend. Three good shows and you could hand over six payments to Ralph Bell by Monday.

JO.   Well that sure as hell would make him sit up and take notice.

MO.   Yeah, I'm encouraged.

MICKEY.   Course it'd be good if they played country, Mo. Or did you forget that part?

MO.   I just wanna help. I'm tryin' really hard not to get distracted.

JO.   Now come on. Mickey didn't mean nothin' by it. Did ya, Mickey?

MICKEY.   No, I didn't.

JO.   She can't help herself, Mo. Just like her mama. Cranky by nature.

MO.   Yeah, I suppose you're right.

MICKEY.   You done real good with that numbers stuff, Mo.

JO.   All right. Now we all got plenty of work to do. I'm gonna need those numbers in writin', Mo.

MO.   You can count on me, Jo. *(Jo exits.)*

MICKEY.   Hey, Mo. I think the singin' went pretty good.

MO.   I still say "suckin' up" is not a nice thing to put in a song. *(Mo exits. Jo and Mickey interrupt the trio as they practice "FROM CHOPIN TO COUNTRY.")*

JO.   So you gals are still here, I see.

MICKEY.   I forgot to tell you, they're still here.

LEE.   Ms. Carlson — if you'd just give us a minute of your time —

JO.   So you've decided you really are the next Mandrel Sisters —

MARY LOU.   Ah — no — that — that wouldn't be right ... did she say madrigal?

LEE.   Yes. Well, we call this uh — classic country ... it's the newest thing.

JO.   I hope so.

LEE.

FROM CHOPIN TO COUNTRY IN ONE SINGLE DAY.

RITA.

FROM CHOPIN TO COUNTRY, THIS TICKET'S ONE WAY.

LEE.

FROM BRANDENBURG,

RITA.

TO BRANDIN' COWS,

MARY LOU.

I COULD HAVE BEEN IN HEIDELBERG BY NOW!

RITA.

FROM CHORALES TO CORRALS, WHO'D EVER HAVE THOUGHT.

(To herself.)

I'M PRAYING TO GOD THAT WE DON'T GET CAUGHT.

LEE.

WE HOPE YOU DON'T KILL US, WE'LL DO THIS SOMEHOW.

MARY LOU.

I COULD HAVE BEEN IN LIECHTENSTEIN BY NOW!

I THINK I HEAR A LARGO,

RITA.

ARRIVING BY WELLS FARGO.

LEE.

I'D RIDE FOR MILES BY PONY

MARY LOU.

JUST TO HEAR A SYMPHONY.

RITA.

FROM CHOPIN TO COUNTRY IT HAPPENED SO FAST.

MARY LOU.

I HOPE I'M ASLEEP AND THIS NIGHTMARE WON'T LAST.

LEE.

LET'S ROUND UP SOME "DOGIES".

RITA.

LET'S GO SLOP A SOW.

MARY LOU.

I COULD HAVE BEEN IN DÜSSELDORF BY NOW.

SO I'LL JUST PLAY PARTITAS

RITA.

WHILE REDNECKS EAT FAJITAS.

LEE.

TOP OFF YOUR TEXAS WIENIE

MARY LOU.

WITH KETCHUP AND PUCCINI.

TRIO.

FROM CHOPIN TO COUNTRY,

IT'S REALLY QUITE PERFUNCT'RY.

WE'RE SO GLAD TO BE HERE, WE'RE TICKLED AND HOW.

LEE.

I COULD HAVE BEEN IN HEIDELBERG,

RITA.

I COULD HAVE BEEN IN LIECHTENSTEIN,

MARY LOU.

I COULD HAVE BEEN IN DÜSSELDORF,

TRIO.

BY NOW!

MICKEY.   Should we get the chicken wire, Jo?

LEE.   Chicken wire?

JO.   Keep ya'll from gettin' hit by the bottles and food. See, we nail a chicken wire screen across the front of the stage when we expect a crowd to be rowdy ... or mean.

MARY LOU.   I'm sorry, you said bottles ... and food?

LEE.   We've had difficult audiences before.

MARY LOU.   Bottles and food!?

JO.   Oh, this is crazy! Look gals, I'm sure you're perfectly well liked people in your own country but it ain't gonna wash in Kansas.

MARY LOU.   Miss Carlson — we've committed ourselves to this ... we — we sang our solidarity song.

MICKEY.   Ask 'em to sing it again, Jo. *(To S.A.I. tune.)* "Sigma, Tanya and Wynona ..." *(Mickey exits.)*

RITA.   Give us a chance. We're good musicians, we can do this —

JO.   We're talkin' country, ladies. It ain't just a bunch of notes strung together, it's a feelin'. And if you don't got it, you can't give it — and, well — ya'll don't got it. And, quite frankly, if you don't give it, *(She refers to the audience.)* they don't get it. And if they don't get it, they don't just go home, they throw bottles.

MARY LOU.   — and food! What kind of food?

LEE.   We can do this.

JO.   Ever been on the wrong end of a beer bottle?

MARY LOU.   Or a corn dog?

JO.   Generally speaking, an unpleasant experience.... Ain't no way in hell I'm lettin' you gals on this stage tomorrow night.

RITA.   We can get it.

LEE.   Give us the day — make your decision then.

MARY LOU.   What do you mean — "a feeling"? Of course it's a series of notes strung together. It's music.

JO.   Ladies, you ain't listenin'.... Oh! The things we do! *(Jo, on piano, begins "KINGDOM OF COUNTRY.")*

FATHER GAMBLED 'WAY OUR SAVINGS.

MOTHER HAD TO SELL HER HAIR.

PREACHERS GAVE THE SAME OLD ANSWERS,

"SOMETIMES LIFE DON'T TREAT YA FAIR."

ALWAYS KNEW WAS SOMETHIN' BETTER,

WOULD GET THERE THROUGH MY FAITH AND PRAYER.

THEN I FOUND MY CHURCH OF REFUGE,

COUNTRY MUSIC GOT ME THERE.

(Chorus.)

THOU SHALT NOT WHINE IN THE KINGDOM OF COUNTRY.

VENGEANCE IS MINE IN THE KINGDOM OF SONG.

AND IF YOU GET THERE, YOU'LL SURELY KNOW IT,

DON'T BLOW IT.

BLESSED ARE THE PICKERS,

NOT THE CITY SLICKERS,

IT'S THE PLACE WHERE I BELONG.

(Rita takes over playing piano.) Get in here, honey. Play it from the heart!

IN THE LAND WITHOUT MY MUSIC

MISERY WAS MY ONLY FRIEND.

MY MOUTH AROUND A SHOTGUN BARREL

SEEMED THE ONLY WAY IT'D END.

NOW THE VIPERS THAT SURROUND ME

WEAR SUITS WITH TIES AND GOLDEN CHAINS.

TELLIN' ME MY KIND OF MUSIC

WILL NEVER TOP THE CHARTS AGAIN.

(Repeat chorus. The women sing back up.)

YOU RISE AGAIN IN THE KINGDOM OF COUNTRY.

SURPRISIN' THEM, IN THE KINGDOM OF SONG.

AND LIKE OLD THOMAS YOU MUSN'T DOUBT IT —

JUST SHOUT IT.

GET BEHIND ME SATAN.

THE REST OF LIFE IS WAITIN'.

IT'S THE PLACE WHERE I AM STRONG —

I AM STRONG

Now *that's* country.

MARY LOU.   It certainly is.

RITA.   That was amazing, Jo —

LEE.   Why are you looking for somebody else to do your reopening?!

JO.   'Cause I ain't singin' on stage — end of story.

LEE. Did you write that song too?

JO. My mama wrote it — now why don't you ladies try payin' a little more attention to yourselves and a little less to me. *(Mo enters, crosses to jukebox and selects a song. Within the scene that follows is a duel of musical quotes between the Trio and Mickey at the jukebox. Quotes are derived from familiar country and classical pieces. The first suggested duel is "D-I-V-O-R-C-E" answered with "Fur Elyse."*)*

MO. Hey Jo, I found some more of them old pictures of girl singers you were lookin' for.

JO. Good work, Mo. Let's get 'em hung up. *(Jukebox begins to play.)*

LEE. Listen … listen to that. Doesn't it sound familiar?

RITA. Fur Elyse!!

LEE. That's what I thought! *(Mickey kicks the jukebox off, and the Trio responds.)*

MICKEY. This is blasphemy!

LEE. Mickey, all popular music is derived from the classics.

MICKEY. Oh, really? *(Mickey returns to the jukebox, pushes another button. The suggested song, "Walkin' After Midnight"* plays for a couple of bars. She kicks it off. The Trio responds by playing a couple bars of "Waltz of the Flowers."* Mickey pushes another button and a couple bars of "I Fall to Pieces"* plays. She kicks it off. Mary Lou responds by playing "Czardas"* on the violin. Mickey pushes another button and a couple bars of "Home on the Range"* plays. She kicks it off. The Trio sings "Pre des Ramparts de Sevilla"* from* Carmen. *Mickey takes an extra moment to select the next tune. She pushes a button and the suggested song, "Achey Breaky Heart"* begins to play. The Trio look at each other as they puzzle over the tune, take a beat, then turn to Mickey and shake their heads in defeat. Mickey lets out a victory cry and she and Mo line dance out the kitchen door.)*

MARY LOU. *(To Lee.)* Make it stop! RUN! *(Lee shuts the jukebox off.)*

LEE. What do you say, Ms. Carlson? Will you give us a shot?

JO. "Can't break a bronco less it's buckin' …"

LEE. I'm sorry?

JO. That's what my Mama always said.

RITA. And what did she mean?

JO. You got your chance, ladies.

LEE and RITA. Great!

MARY LOU. "Don't put your hand on a hot stove."

LEE. What?

MARY LOU. That's what my mother always said.

* See Special Note on Songs and Recordings on copyright page.

JO.   Go do something, ladies, before I change my mind. Put that fancy education to some use. You read music, don't ya?

MARY LOU.   Of course we do.

JO.   There's trunks full of music backstage — I said GO! And find yourselves somethin' decent to wear.

MARY LOU.   Oh, we have our blacks.

JO.   And come Sunday mornin', you might just be wearin' 'em. But tomorrow night, we're talkin' fringe.

RITA.   Fringe!!

LEE.   We're gonna play!!!

JO.   You've got one hour to come up with a decent 20 minute set.

LEE and RITA.   OK! *(Lee and Rita exit. Mary Lou has begun to play carefully and quietly through "Kingdom of Country." Jo listens for a bit.)*

JO.   You're not gonna go find yourself an outfit?

MARY LOU.   The fringe won't matter much if I can't play the music.

JO.   You play that fiddle like there's a gun to your head.

MARY LOU.   It's a violin.

JO.   Oh, pardon me … didn't know there was a difference …

MARY LOU.   Of course there's a difference … there must be.

JO.   How do you fit that "violin" under your chin with that great big ole chip on your shoulder?

MARY LOU.   It wasn't a problem at Carnegie Hall.

JO.   You don't say? *(Mary Lou begins Mozart Violin Concerto No. 3. Her shoulder seizes and her bow screeches across the strings.)* How come your head jerks like that when you play the fiddle?

MARY LOU.   It's a pinched nerve.

JO.   Somethin's pinched, I'll grant ya that.

MARY LOU.   Thank you, Ms. Carlson, for an experience which I will not soon forget. Please extend my heartfelt wishes to Rita and Lee for a rousing and truly unruly opening night. Complete with bottles and food.

JO.   Didn't you sing some secret song — promised you'd stay … somethin' like that? You ever try a mandolin?

MARY LOU.   Excuse me?

JO.   Mandolin? It's strung just like a fiddle.

MARY LOU.   Certainly I am familiar with the instrument as would be any Coghill graduate.

JO.   You know the more I talk to you the less I like you.

MARY LOU.   Then why do you insist on continuing?

JO.   Because you're the only one in this little band who has the slightest hope of gettin' the feelin'.

MARY LOU.   I'm afraid you couldn't be more wrong, Ms. Carlson! I'm not the slightest bit interested in your ... type ... of music.

JO.   Hell, you're wound so tight, you're makin' the air vibrate.

MARY LOU. . What?

JO.   Sooner or later you're gonna explode and when you do you'll have 'em hangin' from the rafters, Miss Mary Lou. That's that feelin' I been talkin' about.

MARY LOU.   I don't WANT that feeling.

JO.   That's all right. You don't get it when you WANT it. You get it when you NEED it.

MARY LOU.   I've been playing the classics since I was old enough to hold a bow.

JO.   So was it your mama started you off with the fidd— violin?

MARY LOU.   It's really none of your business.

JO.   No, I suppose it's not. (*Jo starts to leave.*)

MARY LOU.   Wait. I'm sorry ... you have me very confused.

JO.   My mama gave me the music too. In fact, she taught me everything I love ... cookin', poker, singin'.

MARY LOU.   My mother had a maid and I don't think she knew much about poker.

JO.   What's the first song she ever taught you? (*On Mandolin, Mary Lou plays the first few notes of "Old Rugged Cross.")* Well, hell's bells! Same song my mama taught me. I was barely three years old! (*Jo, on guitar, segues into the beginning of "SONGS MY MAMA SANG."*)

> SOMETIMES AT NIGHT AS I'M GOING TO BED,
>
> SONGS FROM MY CHILDHOOD FLOOD INTO MY HEAD.
>
> HYMNS ABOUT JESUS AND FISHES AND BREAD —
>
> MOTHER TAUGHT EACH ONE TO ME.

* See Special Note on Songs and Recordings on copyright page.

(Chorus.)

MAMA, MAMA, SING ME A SONG.

SHE PLAYED THE PIANO AND SHE PLAYED SOME NOTES WRONG.

MAMA, MAMA, SO GENTLE YET STRONG —

I SEE HER KIND HANDS ON THE KEYS

HOW I CHERISH THE TIME THAT WE SPENT.

OH HOW QUICKLY THOSE YEARS CAME AND WENT.

WHEN I SAT ON MY DEAR MOTHER'S KNEE

AND SHE SANG ALL THOSE SWEET SONGS TO ME

(Instrumental: guitar and mandolin.)

(Chorus. Mary Lou joins in.)

SING ME YOUR SONGS,

SING ME YOUR SONGS,

SING ME THOSE SWEET MELODIES.

Thanks, Mary Lou, pleasure singin' with you. You ever get the feelin' that some people keep the best part of themselves all locked up?

MARY LOU.   Uuuhhhh … *(Rita and Lee enter complete with super-bouffed wigs. Rita carries a song sheet. Lee carries a guitar.)*

RITA.   *(À la Minnie Pearl.)* How-dee!

JO.   Lord God!

LEE.   I can hear my truck crashin' and my dog dyin' already!

RITA.   The higher the hair — the closer to God.

JO.   There is something seriously wrong with you ladies.

RITA.   This little ole song was written by Jo Carlson…. Cut 'er loose, Lee! *(Lee, with Rita, sings "HEADS OR TAILS.")*

LEE.

ME AND RUBY FLIPPED A QUARTER TO SEE WHO GOT HIS TABLE,

WHEN THAT TAN AND LANKY TRUCKER SAUNTERED INTO
    MABEL'S —

THE ONLY DINER BETWEEN COLBY AND THE COLORADO BORDER —

I CALLED "TAILS" TO WIN THE PRIZE OF SAYIN' "MAY I TAKE YOUR
    ORDER."

THAT ONE-EYED EAGLE SMILED UP AT ME FROM RUBY'S WRIST.

SHE SAID, "3 OUT OF 5," I SAID "NO" —

RITA.

BOY WAS SHE PISSED.

LEE.

AS I AMBLED TOWARDS HIS TABLE WITH MY ORDER PAD AND BIC,

I SAID, "HI, MY NAME IS JOSIE," HE WINKED

RITA.

AND JUST SAID "DICK".

LEE and RITA.   *(Chorus.)*

YOU KNOW IT NEVER FAILS

WITH LOVE IT'S HEADS OR IT'S TAILS.

THE FLIP OF A COIN,

A TWITCH IN THE GROIN,

OH, THE GAMBLE OF LOVE.

JO.   Where's the mandolin?! *(Mary Lou joins in on mandolin.)*

LEE and RITA.

OH, THE FIRST MONTHS WE WERE HAPPY, NOT A CROSS WORD OR
A FIGHT

BUT THEN HE STARTED GAMBLIN' AND DRINKIN' EVERY NIGHT.

HE'D COME HOME DRUNK, CRAWL INTO BED, HE ALWAYS
SMELLED OF GIN.

I'D CRY MYSELF TO SLEEP THINKING HOW GOOD IT ONCE HAD
BEEN.

BABY, DID YOU MEAN IT WHEN YOU KISSED ME TENDERLY?

AND HONEY, WHEN WE MADE LOVE, DID YOU KNOW THAT IT WAS
ME?

WHY WAS, "DARLIN', I SURE LOVE YOU" SO HARD FOR YOU TO SAY?

DICK, I HAD TO LEAVE YOU 'CAUSE I'D A DIED IF I HAD STAYED.

YOU KNOW IT NEVER FAILS

WITH LOVE IT'S HEADS OR IT'S TAILS.

THE FLIP OF A COIN,

A TWITCH IN THE GROIN,

OH THE GAMBLE OF LOVE.

A FLIP OF A COIN,

A TWITCH IN THE GROIN,

OH THE GAMBLE OF LOVE.

JO.   Funny — I never quite heard it that way in my head ... but you're better than you were.

MARY LOU.   What a thoroughly depressing song.

LEE.   Yeah? Made me feel better than I've felt in months.

RITA.   Sometimes there's nothing more uplifting than someone else who's more depressed ... I think I'll call Bob. *(Mo enters.)*

JO.   Hold up, ladies, we got a lot of work to do!

MO.   They gotta get some supper first, Jo.

JO.   Mo, we got a deadline here! Let's get on with it! *(Mo exits.)*

RITA.   Do I have time to call my husband?

JO.   You got five minutes. Go ahead. *(She turns to Lee.)* Now's the time. You got a husband or boyfriend? Call 'im now.

LEE.   *(Caught off-guard, forced to decide if she will "out" herself here.)* I'm ... uh ... *(Deciding to say nothing.)* OK. Thanks. *(Jo exits.)*

RITA.   So. Who you gonna call? Your husband or your boyfriend?

LEE.   I'm calling your sister. *(Mo enters.)*

MO.   LADIES!! WE'VE GOT A DEADLINE HERE!! *(Mo exits. Mary Lou on violin, Lee on guitar — the sounds transform from tuning and odd chords to "LOVE'S SORROW.")*

JO.

A GIRL IN A RED DRESS WITH A BIG GUITAR —

SHE WAS ONLY 16 WHEN SHE WALKED IN THIS BAR.

DADDY KNEW SHE WAS GOOD AND SOMEDAY SHE'D GO FAR

BUT NOT SO FAR THAT SHE'D LEAVE.

(The melody is picked up in the violin part — underscoring dialogue and song.) Mama take me with you! "I'm sorry Josie, I can't."

> YOU SAID THAT A LIFE ON THE ROAD WOULDN'T BE
>
> THE KIND OF A CHILDHOOD YOU'D INTENDED FOR ME.
>
> SO YOU LEFT ME WITH PAPA AND SET YOURSELF FREE.
>
> I CAN'T SAY I BLAME YOU FOR ACTING SO SELFISHLY.

RITA.   Bob!

> I HAD TO GO, YOU KNOW, I'M NOT COLD.
>
> I HAD TO TRY BEFORE I GOT OLD.
>
> STOP TELLING ME SO VERY RATIONALLY
>
> TO HAVE A CHILD AND SET PRIORITIES.
>
> IT'S MY LIFE TOO, YOU KNOW I WON'T BREAK.
>
> I'M DOING THIS FOR YOUR AND MY SAKE.
>
> I FEEL I'LL LOSE PART OF MYSELF
>
> IF YOU JUST PUT ME ON THE MOMMY SHELF.

LEE.

> I CAN'T KEEP ON LIVING ON THE EDGES OF LIFE,
>
> ALWAYS EXPLAINING WHY I'M NOT SOMEONE'S WIFE.
>
> CHANGING THE PRONOUNS TO PUT OTHERS AT EASE —
>
> THANK GOD FOR THE MUSIC AND OLD FRIENDS LIKE THESE.

JO.   Daddy!

> YOU LOST ME MY MOTHER, I'VE FORGOTTEN HER FACE!
>
> AND NOW FROM THE GRAVE, YOU'VE LOST ME THIS PLACE.
>
> OLD MAN, THIS WASN'T YOUR PLAN,
>
> I'LL DO ALL I CAN,
>
> IT'S IN MY HANDS.

RITA.

> IT'S MY LIFE TOO, YOU KNOW I WON'T BREAK.

JO.

> MAMA STAY.

RITA.

I'M DOING THIS FOR YOUR AND MY SAKE.

LEE.

OH, ONE DAY.

RITA, LEE and JO.

I FEEL I'LL LOSE PART OF MYSELF,

IF I DON'T GET DOWN FROM THIS SHELF.

(Mary Lou begins "LOOKING FOR A MIRACLE.")

MARY LOU.

MY VIOLIN TEACHER CLIPPED MY NAILS 'TIL THEY BLED.

I PRACTICED FOR THREE HOURS AFTER DINNER THEN TO BED,

"YOU'RE GOOD ENOUGH TO MAKE IT BIG" HE SAID.

Too bad you're a woman, you could have been a conductor.

OUR MOTHERS ARE JUST HOUSEWIVES WHEN THEY COOK FOR A
LIVING

IF OUR FATHERS DID IT, THEY'D CALL HIM A CHEF.

WHY ARE WE THE ONES WHO HAVE TO BE SO SELFLESS AND
FORGIVING?

WHY WEREN'T WE THE COMPOSERS OF THE CLASSICS?

CLIPPING COUPONS FOR COLD VLASSICS ISN'T MY IDEA OF ...

OR AM I JUST LOOKING FOR A MIRACLE

LONGING FOR A DAY THAT MAY NEVER COME.

ALWAYS HEARING SOMEONE SAY

THAT THEY'VE GOT A BETTER WAY

TO DO ALL THE THINGS I'VE DONE.

MAYBE I SHOULD PRAY FOR A MIRACLE,

WHEN I'LL FINALLY KNOW WHAT ALL THIS IS FOR.

DID I DO IT ALL FOR MOM?

STILL KEEP GOING THOUGH SHE'S GONE —

POUNDING ON A SILENT DOOR.

SOMEONE LET ME IN,

I'VE BEEN OUT HERE FOR YEARS.

IT'S DARK AND LONELY

BUT I'LL NEVER LET YOU SEE MY TEARS.

MIRACLES, MIRACLES, WAITING TO BEGIN.

(Cadenza.)

JO.

OR AM I JUST LOOKING FOR A MIRACLE

LONGING FOR A DAY THAT MAY NEVER COME.

ALWAYS HEARING SOMEONE SAY

THAT THEY'VE GOT A BETTER WAY

TO DO ALL THE THINGS I'VE DONE.

ENTIRE COMPANY.

I'LL JUST KEEP ON HOPING FOR MY/A MIRACLE

HOPING FOR THAT TIME WHEN I ASK FOR MORE.

THEN I'LL FINALLY HAVE THE NERVE

TO DEMAND WHAT I DESERVE.

I ONLY HOPE, I'LL REALIZE

I'VE FOUND WHAT I'VE BEEN SEARCHING FOR.

JO.

OR AM I JUST LOOKING FOR A MIRACLE?

BLACKOUT

ACT TWO

It is early morning on Saturday. The bar has gone through a few decor changes and is almost ready for the show. However, a few details remain undone. Picture frames sit on the steps to Jo's office. Mickey and Mo enter.

MICKEY.   JO CARLSON!!!!! JO CARLSON!! *(Jo enters, nearly tripping over the picture frames.)*

JO.   What in the hell?! Who's makin' that racket?! Damnit!! Somebody hang these pictures before I break my neck!!

MICKEY.   It's Mickey and Mo and we ain't leavin'.

JO.   Good, 'cause you start work in 15 minutes.

MO.   That's not what she meant … is that what you meant?

MICKEY.   No, it is not.

MO.   That's what I thought … that's not what she meant …

MICKEY.   I've kept pretty much silent about these three wackos you brought in for the openin' — but I just can't do it anymore. I want my chance!! All my life I been wantin' to be on this stage and I'm really hurt you didn't even ask us to audition!

MO.   Yeah! What she said.

MICKEY.   So I'm not leavin' 'til you give us an audition.

JO.   How long are you willing to wait?

MO.   Well, I gotta be at work in 15 minutes.

MICKEY.   Mo. You are at work.

MO.   Right. Oh. Oh!! So then I can come back tomorrow.

MICKEY.   You gotta give us a listen, Jo.

MO.   Please.

JO.   Oh, good God, so sing already. *(Mickey and Mo stare blankly.)* SING!

MICKEY.   Set me up, Mo!! *(Mickey gets the banjo. Mo prepares the stage and gets the bucket and brushes.)* How's my hair? *(Mo gives the thumbs up. Mickey starts to play.)*

MO.   Wait!

MICKEY.   What?! *(Mo presents a cowgirl hat obviously decorated for Mickey.)*

MO.   I made you a hat. *(Mickey starts to plays again.)* Wait!!

MICKEY.   What?!?! *(Mo exits and reenters pulling a home-made, life-size cow on a rope.)*

MO.   I made you a cow. *(Mickey begins playing again, then she stops herself.)*

MICKEY.   Is that it?

MO.   That's it. *(Mickey begins again and this time, actually continues.)*

MICKEY.

> I LOOK AT ALL THEM PICTURES IN THE MAGAZINES
>
> WHERE THEY SHOW YOU ALL THE MODELS IN DESIGNER JEANS.
>
> ALL THE GIRLS ARE SKINNY AND THEIR HAIR IS FLAT —
>
> WHY WOULD I WANT TO LOOK LIKE THAT?
>
> I LIKE THE FASHIONS DON'TS AND NOT THE DO'S.
>
> I READ THE COMICS AND I THROW AWAY THE NEWS.
>
> CITY FOLKS LAUGH AT MY K-MART CLOTHES
>
> BUT I GOT MY OWN STYLE

MO.

> AND SHE'S GOT HER OWN NOSE.

MICKEY.

> TWELVE STEP PROGRAMS MAKE ME YAWN

MO.

> BUT SHE COULD TWO STEP ALL NIGHT LONG.

MICKEY.

> PINK FLAMINGOS ON MY LAWN.
>
> BUT DON'T CALL ME TRAILER TRASH,

MO.

> SHE LIVES IN A MOBILE HOME

MICKEY.

> YOU CAN ALWAYS KEEP ME DOWN ON THE FARM
>
> 'CAUSE I'VE ALWAYS LIKED A MAN WITH A HALF-TAN ARM.
>
> A PICK-UP TRUCK WITH OVER-SIZED TIRES
>
> MAKES ME WEAK IN THE KNEES, SETS MY HEART ON FIRE.

MO.

    CHEESE FRIES, WISE GUYS, DEMOLITION DERBY

MICKEY.

    STIR FRIES, NICE GUYS DO NOTHIN' FER ME.

    NEVER CUT OUT GOURMET RECIPES.

MO.

    SHE PREFERS THE CUISINE AT THE TASTY FREEZE.

MICKEY.

    I LIKE A CAR WITH LOTS OF CHROME.

MO.

    I CAN MAKE ART OUT OF STYROFOAM.

MICKEY.

    I AIN'T GOT NO CELLULAR PHONE.

    BUT DON'T CALL ME TRAILER TRASH,

MO.

    SHE LIVES IN A MOBILE HOME.

MICKEY and MO.

    DON'T CALL ME/HER TRAILER TRASH —

MO.

    SHE LIVES IN A MOBILE HOME.

MICKEY.   What do you say, Jo?!!

MO.   Yeah! What?

JO.   Puts to rest any questions I might have had.

MICKEY.   Will you give us a shot, Jo?!

MO.   So when do we start?!

JO.   Now. And don't forget to mop behind the bar.

MICKEY.   So I'm not playin' tonight?

JO.   Not tonight ...

MICKEY.   Why won't you let me on stage, Jo?!

JO.   You ain't ready, Mickey.

MICKEY.   I'm sure as hell as ready as that wacko with the vi-o-lin.

JO.   You ain't got time to sing, you got mouths to feed.

MICKEY.   Not every mama who sings walks out on her kids!

MO.   Mickey!

MICKEY.   Ain't no different from your daddy! *(Mickey exits.)*

MO.   She didn't mean it, Jo. *(Mo exits. Rita and Lee enter.)*

LEE.   Hey, Jo! We got three tunes memorized.

JO.   Get set up, girls. I'll be back. *(Jo calls after Mickey.)* Mickey? *(She exits.)*

RITA.   Just a quick phone call.

LEE.   You've got to put him out of your mind. Besides, I'm sure he'll call. The man is a trumpet player, Rita. They're not the most dependable people.

RITA.   At least he's not a drummer.

LEE.   That was a study in rhythm. *(Mary Lou enters.)*

MARY LOU.   You're finally here. What's so funny?

RITA.   We're reviewing Lee's romantic history.

MARY LOU.   Do we have time?

LEE.   Well at least *I* can say that I have *never* sucked the lips that have sucked a bassoon.

MARY LOU.   He was a good person.

LEE.   I shouldn't date musicians anymore. It's probably healthier.

RITA.   What is it about a good musician? They can look like Quasimodo at the dinner table but put a horn in their hands or sit them behind a keyboard and suddenly you're looking at the most sexually irresistible person on the planet. What is that?

LEE.   Maybe they feel sexier when they're playing.

MARY LOU.   You're wrong. The *music* is sex. Not the player.

RITA.   Mary Lou!

MARY LOU.   Beethoven's Sixth is an orgy for God's sake!! What album do you put on when you have a date?

LEE.   She may be right. I don't think I've ever tried to seduce someone over dinner, candlelight and Hooked on Phonics.

RITA.   Worked for me.

MARY LOU.   No! It's the music. Rachmaninoff ... no ... Chopin's "Revolutionary Etude." *(Rita starts playing "the" section of the "Etude" which has an "orgasmic" effect on Mary Lou.)* STOP! We don't have time for this! We're in real trouble here!

RITA.   No, we're not.

MARY LOU.   We're not?!

RITA.   I've been inspired by this place.

LEE.   What do you mean?

RITA.   Well, all I do back home is teach kids all day. I know it's important but it's not very exciting. You'll both probably think I'm crazy but I went down to the Shakey's Pizza Parlor near us to audition to be one of those saloon piano players.

MARY LOU.   No.

RITA.   You know, they wear those Miss Kitty-looking costumes — fake beauty marks, false eyelashes, little feather things in their hair ... I didn't get the job. And I *really* wanted it!

MARY LOU.   Why?

RITA.   Because it wasn't me.

COULDA BEEN VAN CLIBURN,

LIBERACE WITH HIS SIDEBURNS,

COULDA BEEN A. RUBENSTEIN.

I'D TRADE ANY OF THOSE MISTERS

FOR THE LENNON SISTERS

'CAUSE JOANNE CASTLE ALWAYS WAS A HERO OF MINE.

MARY LOU.   From Lawrence Welk?

RITA.

I WANNA BE A HONKY TONK GIRL NOT SOME EVERYDAY PIANO
   MARM.

THOUGH CLASSICALLY TRAINED, I STUDIED AND STRAINED TO BE
   DEMURE.

BUT I LOVED TICKLIN' THOSE KEYS, BOUNCIN' MY KNEES,
   JIGGLIN' MY ARMS.

NAILING THUMBTACKS ON THE HAMMERS SO I WOULD SOUND
   JUST LIKE HER.

(Piano break.)

YOU ASK ME, "WHY WOULD YOU DO IT, IT'S SO DEGRADING?"

I ANSWER, "COULD'VE PLAYED ACCORDION SO I'M CELEBRATING..."

(Jo enters and watches.)

THAT I'M A HONKY TONK GIRL, PLAYIN' CLASSICS WITHOUT CLASS.

WHEN I'M DOWN ON MY LUCK, I'LL PLAY FOR A — BUCK —

WHATEVER THEY DROP IN MY GLASS.

'CAUSE I'LL BE WORKIN' FOR MYSELF AND MAKIN' MY OWN PAY,

I WOULDN'T THINK OF LIVING MY LIFE ANY OTHER WAY

THAN A HONKY TONK, A HONKY TONK GIRL.

MARY LOU.   Wow — I didn't know you could do that, Rita.

RITA.   Call me Kitty.

JO.   Well, knock me over with a feather. I feel a revelation comin' on. You're closin' in on it, ladies, but you gotta understand that it ain't just the singin'. It's what you say while you're singin' it. It's your toe-tappin', it's a low-slung guitar ... it's the way ya eye-ball 'em in the back row. *(Beat.)* All right, who wants to go first? *(There are no takers.)* OK Lee, it's show time. Get the music stand. Here's the music. I'll give ya a couple measures — then you come in — *(Jo, on piano, begins "EVERY SATURDAY NIGHT.")*

LEE.   *(With painstaking enunciation.)*

IN A LITTLE TOWN CALLED MUD ROCK CREEK NEAR NASHVILLE, TENNESSEE

I WAS BORN TO MY DEAR MAMA, I WAS ONE OF TWENTY-THREE.

OUR LIFE WAS NEVER EASY BUT OUR HOUSE WAS FULL OF SONG.

MAMA SAID THAT IF YOU'RE SINGIN' LIFE DOESN'T SEEM SO WRONG.

JO.   OK. You're workin' too hard. Think of easin' into a hot-tub not jumpin' into a cold crick! Slide, ladies, slide. Rita! Front and center!

RITA.   *(Sliding up to every note.)*

I'D CAREFULLY SAVE MY PENNIES, FOR MONEY WAS ALWAYS TIGHT,

TO SEE THE GRAND OLE OPRY EACH AND EVERY SATURDAY NIGHT.

I LOVED THE STARS I HEARD THERE, LIKE LORETTA, DOLLY AND ROY.

I DREAMT THAT MAYBE SOMEDAY I'D BRING OTHERS THAT SAME JOY.

JO.   Think of the music as your road map, ladies, not your Bible. You don't have to sing every single solitary note. *(The women don't get it.)* It's your general directions; you know you gotta get from Colby to Rexford — you gotta head east on 24, then north on 83 — but nobody's tellin' ya what kinda car to drive, how to handle a curve or when to stop for lunch. *(They still don't get it.)* It's like this. *(From singing to spoken word, highly interpretive.)*

> I LOVED THE STARS I HEARD THERE, LIKE LORETTA, DOLLY AND
>   ROY.

> I DREAMT THAT MAYBE SOMEDAY I'D BRING OTHERS THAT SAME
>   JOY.

OK now everybody sing. And Mary Lou, I want some fiddle in between!

ALL.

> EVERY SATURDAY NIGHT RIGHT AT FIVE TWENTY-TWO

> ON ROUTE 50 MY JOURNEY WOULD START.

> MY PENNIES AND NICKELS WERE TUCKED IN MY SHOE

> AND A NASHVILLE SONG TUCKED IN MY HEART.

(Mary Lou breaks into the Mendelssohn violin concerto.)

JO.   Mary LOU!!!!! *(Mary Lou stops playing.)* Lee! Next verse!

LEE.   *(Spoken.)*

> I WAS MARRIED TO LOVIN' BOBBY JOE IN THE SUMMER OF '69

> BUT SOON OUR JOY WAS ENDED I LOST THAT MAN OF MINE

JO.   You gotta sing *some* of it, honey!!

LEE.   *(Sings.)*

> A LETTER CAME FROM UNCLE SAM, ADDRESSED TO BOBBY JOE

(Speaks.)

> THEY NEEDED HIM IN VIET NAM AND BOBBY SAID HE'D GO.

JO.   That's it! Rita! *(Rita is better by this verse.)*

RITA.

> NEVER AGAIN WAS I TO HOLD MY BOBBY TENDERLY

> BUT THERE WAS SOMETHING LEFT OF HIM TWAS BOBBY'S LEGACY.

> THAT SPRING I HAD HIS BABY, HE WAS SO CUTE SO BRIGHT

> AND HE CAME WITH ME TO NASHVILLE EACH AND EVERY SATUR-
>   DAY NIGHT.

JO. I wanna see you movin', ladies!

ALL.

> EVERY SATURDAY NIGHT RIGHT AT FIVE TWENTY-TWO
>
> ON ROUTE 50 MY JOURNEY WOULD START.
>
> MY PENNIES AND NICKELS WERE TUCKED IN MY SHOE
>
> AND A NASHVILLE SONG TUCKED IN MY HEART.

JO. Mary Lou!

MARY LOU.

> AND THEN ONE NIGHT, ONE AWFUL NIGHT, FATE DEALT
>   ANOTHER BLOW.
>
> WHILE HITCHIN' INTO NASHVILLE I LOST LITTLE BOBBY JOE.
>
> A SEMI-TRUCK CAME ROUND A CURVE, THE WEATHER THAT
>   NIGHT WAS BAD —
>
> GOD DECIDED THAT BOBBY JR. SHOULD BE UP THERE WITH DAD.

(Mary Lou choked up, blows her nose.)

RITA and LEE. Allergies. *(Jo comes in to finish the verse.)*

JO.

> SO NOW I AM A SINGER, NOT A MOTHER OR HOUSEWIFE
>
> AND BRINGING JOY TO OTHERS IS THE PURPOSE OF MY LIFE.
>
> THOUGH I HAVE CHANGED IN MANY WAYS, I SOMEHOW DON'T
>   FEEL RIGHT,
>
> IF I DON'T SEE THE OPRY EACH AND EVERY SATURDAY NIGHT.

RITA, LEE and MARY LOU.

> EVERY SATURDAY NIGHT RIGHT AT FIVE TWENTY-TWO
>
> ON ROUTE 50 MY JOURNEY WOULD START.
>
> MY PENNIES AND NICKELS WERE TUCKED IN MY SHOE
>
> AND A NASHVILLE SONG TUCKED IN MY HEART.

(Mary Lou attempts to end with the fiddle, almost succeeding but getting tangled up by the end, finishing with a wavering final note. Jo heads for the door.)

JO. YeeeHa!!!

RITA. Where you going, Jo?

JO. Time for another chat with ol' Ralph Bell. I do believe I just found me some collateral. *(Jo exits.)*

LEE.   That was great!

RITA.   I know I screwed up — getting us booked in here — but you gotta admit, it's a pretty good mistake.

LEE.   There are no mistakes.

MARY LOU.   I think there are mistakes.

LEE.   Mary Lou, aren't you feeling more confident about this than you were yesterday? I thought we sounded pretty good just then.

MARY LOU.   *You* sounded good — *Rita* could obviously be a regular here — but *I* am not going to be able to do this. That's what I've been trying to tell you — I practiced all night ... I really tried ...

RITA.   It's just a bunch of tricks, Mary Lou.

LEE.   You're scared. Think of it as a free-fall and — let go. You've just got to believe you can do it, Mary Lou. You know my family — they're all jocks, right? My Dad's a coach, both my brothers were champion gymnasts. I tried to keep up with them but I'm just not naturally athletic — which is a sad, sad thing for a lesbian. Anyway, the point is, I felt left out and my parents *never* picked up on it. But there *was* one person who did — and do you know what she would have said right now?

MARY LOU.   What?

LEE.   "Don't look down."

MARY LOU.   What's that supposed to mean?

LEE.

> THEY FLEW THROUGH THE AIR WITH THE GREATEST OF EASE —
>
> MY BROTHERS WERE NATURALS ON THE FLYING TRAPEZE.
>
> I STOOD LOOKING DOWN AT MY SMALL TREMBLING KNEES.
>
> GRANDMA KNELT DOWN BESIDE ME AND SAID,

(Chorus.)

> "DON'T LOOK DOWN, THAT'S NOT WHERE YOU'RE GONNA GO.
>
> LOOK STRAIGHT AHEAD NOT THE NET BELOW.
>
> YOU'RE THE BRAVEST GIRL THAT I KNOW.
>
> DON'T LOOK DOWN, EVEN THOUGH YOU ARE TERRIFIED.
>
> MAY WANNA RUN BUT YOU NEEDN'T HIDE
>
> 'CAUSE I'LL BE RIGHT HERE BESIDE YOU."

I THINK THAT I KNEW BY THE TIME I WAS THREE

THAT MEDALS AND TROPHIES WEREN'T THE PRIZES FOR ME.

GRANDMA KNEW IT TOO AND SHE WHISPERED, "LET'S SEE

WHAT SPECIAL THING YOU'RE MEANT TO DO."

SHE BOUGHT ME A CELLO AND MADE NO DEMANDS

SAID "YOU'LL ROSIN A BOW NOW INSTEAD OF YOUR HANDS."

AND STILL WHEN I SEE ALL THOSE FACES BELOW

I CAN HEAR GRANDMA'S VOICE SOFT AND LOW.

(Chorus.)

AND THEN LATE ONE NIGHT, I GOT A TELEPHONE CALL.

MOM SAID GRANDMA WAS SICK AND IN THE HOSPITAL.

WHEN I GOT THERE TO SEE HER SHE LOOKED OH SO SMALL —

I KNEW SHE WAS SLIPPING AWAY.

I STOOD THERE AWHILE BY THE SIDE OF HER BED.

SHE OPENED HER EYES WHEN I KISSED HER FOREHEAD.

I LOOKED DOWN AND CRIED I DIDN'T WANT HER TO SEE —

SHE SMILED AND SHE WHISPERED TO ME,

(Chorus.)

(Jo enters.)

JO.   *(Yelling offstage.)* Don't you ever try and sell this place out from under me again, Ralph Bell! You got a buyer?!?! Send 'em over to the Ball O' Twine!!! MO!!

RITA.   More trouble, Jo?

JO.   Have you *ever* met a more pompous, arrogant son-of-a-bitch than Ralph Bell?! *(Mo enters carrying papers.)*

MARY LOU.   We haven't met Ralph Bell.

MO.   Here're them numbers.

JO.   Where're them numbers?! *(Jo grabs the papers. Mo exits. Jo nearly trips on the pictures still unhung.)* Damnit!! You want somethin' done you gotta do it yourself! *(Jo grabs a picture and hangs it. She stops and stares at it. After a beat, she speaks and then continues to hang the pictures as she talks.)* Texas Ruby. Patsy Montana.

Becky Barfield. Mother Maybelle. Connie Carlson. These are cowgirls, ladies. They didn't play by anyone's rules but their own. They made their own way. Ain't *no* fat, ugly banker would have told any one of them, when or how they would shut down their joint. Do I make myself clear?! They found out for themselves. Blazed their own trail. THAT is where I come from — And I am here to tell you — ain't nobody gonna take that away from me! And they ain't gonna take it away from you either!! Now, we got a long way to go 'fore dark and there's no way we're gonna get there if ya'll don't know where ya came from!
(Jo, on piano, begins "THEY'RE ALL COWGIRLS TO ME." The trio eventually plays along.)

> YOU'VE HEARD ABOUT COWBOYS OF THE WEST —
>
> HOW INJUNS AND OUTLAWS PUT THEIR COURAGE TO THE TEST.
>
> BUT THERE WERE OTHERS WHO FACED THEIR FEARS;
>
> THE FIRST FRONTIER WOMEN PIONEERS.
>
> THEY CAME TO A PLACE CALLED KANSAS.
>
> THEY'D NEVER SEEN A COUNTRYSIDE SO VAST AND STILL.
>
> LIKE PAINTING ON AN EMPTY CANVAS,
>
> THEY LEFT A MASTERPIECE OF WILL.

(Chorus.)

> AND THEY'RE ALL COWGIRLS TO ME
>
> FROM THEIR TAME LIVES THEY CAME HERE TO THE LONE PRAIRIE.
>
> WHERE THE SOUTH WIND BLOWS WILD AND FREE —
>
> THEY'RE ALL GREAT COWGIRLS TO ME.

Mary Lou!! Where's that mandolin?!

> THE WOMEN CAME BY THE THOUSANDS WEST,
>
> FROM MOTHERS TO MADAMES — GAMBLERS, SUFFRAGETTES.
>
> CARRIE NATION, POKER ALICE, BELLE STARR, SUSAN B.
>
> THEIR PASSION — A PRICELESS LEGACY.
>
> THEY CAME TO THIS PLACE CALLED KANSAS.
>
> ONLY THEY COULD TAME A LAND SO WILD AND FREE.
>
> THEY PAINTED BOLDLY ON THIS CANVAS.
>
> THEIR BRUSHES LEFT TO YOU AND ME.

45

Sing!!!

(Chorus.)

(Instrumental.)

(Chorus.)

MARY LOU. *(Very excited.)* So, what you're saying is — is that — well, it's an editorial "they" — "They're all cowgirls" — but what you're actually saying is that *we* — *we* are cowgirls! Yes?

JO. Well —

MARY LOU. Now you know I don't ride — I'm allergic to horses — but OK, yes! Yes! I am a cowgirl! I am a cowgirl!! Yip! Yip!

JO. Cowgirls don't always ride horses to get where they're going — they just *get* where they're going.

MARY LOU. *(Still very excited.)* Come hell or high water!!

JO. Exactly! And right now we're in hell.

LEE. What just happened?

JO. I told Ralph Bell I'd have half his money to him by Monday.

RITA. Is that possible?

JO. *(Referring to Mo's numbers.)* Well according to Mo's figures we need to — *(Clearly the numbers are nearly impossible.)* We need to blow the roof off the place.

LEE. Or what?

JO. Or they padlock the door on Monday morning.

RITA. At least there's no pressure.

MARY LOU. Sounds like a job for COWGIRL!... We gotta sing!... We need a song! Cowgirl need a song!

JO. OK, Cowgirl — I got some ole Zora Layman music upstairs. You woulda liked her — she was a wild woman, just like you, cursin' on her records and callin' her fiddle a violin. Why don't you go on up and get some of that music.

MARY LOU. What a *great* gig! *(Mary Lou exits.)*

JO. She's a peculiar girl.

RITA. So you're not sellin' the place?

JO. Hell, no!

LEE. The Universe provides. *(Mickey and Mo enter.)*

RITA. Yee hah!

LEE.   That a girl, Rita!

MICKEY.   Oh shoot! Which one of you is Rita!?

JO.   You know who they are Mickey — stop being so rude.

RITA.   I'm Rita.

MICKEY.   I forgot to tell you yesterday. Bob, your husband? He called.

RITA.   What did he say?

MICKEY.   He was just returning your call. Oh, and he also said, *(Mickey takes out her order pad and reads:)* "if you wanted to talk to me so badly you should have just stayed at home."

RITA.   Cowgirls didn't have to deal with this.

MO.   They didn't have phones.

MICKEY.   That is exactly right, Mo. Ya'll have got a lot to learn.

JO.   Let 'em alone, Mickey. They have to rehearse.

MICKEY.   Just tryin' to help, Jo. I know it can't be easy turnin' country over-night. Understandin' country music takes a lifetime of sufferin'.

LEE.   I don't think you can get us on the suffering point, Mickey.

MICKEY.   Oh really? How many ex-husbands you got?

LEE.   Do ex-wives count?

MICKEY.   *(To Rita.)* How about you? How many kids will this make?

RITA.   This will make one.

MO.   Tell 'em how many kids you got, Mic.

MICKEY.   Six. Three of 'em came at once. Two of 'em belong to husband number two and one of 'em … well, one of 'em's in reform school. But don't you worry about me 'cause my third husband had insurance that paid real good after the truck wreck. *(Beat.)* Now that's country. *(Mickey exits.)*

LEE.   She could go on Oprah.

MO.   She's been on Oprah. *(Mo exits. Mary Lou appears.)*

JO.   Why, lookee-there. It's Cowgirl. *(Mary Lou, frantic, holds a guitar. She doesn't — can't — speak.)* Well go on, girl! *(Mary Lou falls into "SADDLE TRAMP BLUES" which evolves into a raunchy gyrating performance. Rita will eventually accompany on piano, Lee on tambourine.)*

MARY LOU.

    MY DADDY WAS A COWBOY, MY MAMA WAS A SQUAW.

    MY BEST FRIEND WAS MY PINTO AND NATURE WAS THE LAW.

I GREW UP KNOWIN' NOTHIN' BUT RIDIN' ON THE RANGE.

COULD'VE MARRIED ME A PREACHER BUT IT'S TOO LATE TO
    CHANGE.

(Chorus. Rita joins with piano.)

I'VE GOT THE SADDLE TRAMP BLUES.

I'VE GOT THE SADDLE TRAMP BLUES.

PREFER MY BOOTS TO PRETTY SHOES,

THE OLD TO THE NEW,

THOSE SADDLE TRAMP BLUES.

JO.   I'm hearin' it but I'm not seein' it! *(Mary Lou responds physically.)*

MARY LOU.

SOME PEOPLE THINK IT'S SHOCKING THAT I RIDE WITH ALL
    THESE MEN

BUT THE ODDS ARE TO MY LIKING, TEN ROOSTERS TO ONE HEN.

TELL ME SOMETHIN' LADIES DON'T YOU THINK IT'D BE ALL
    RIGHT

TO HAVE A COWBOY IN YOUR SADDLE WITH A COWPOKE EVERY
    NIGHT?

(Chorus.)

(Mickey and Mo enter. Mickey carries an envelope.)

THE DAY MAY COME UPON ME WHEN I TIRE OF THIS LIFE —

HAVE A COUPLE CHILDREN, BE A MOTHER AND A WIFE,

BUT I DON'T THINK IT'S LIKELY, I'LL CHANGE THAT
    DRASTICALLY —

YOU CAN MAKE THE BABIES, LEAVE THE PRACTICING TO ME.

(Chorus.)

JO.   That's it! There it is!! Rita! Lee! Come on, gals! Follow Mary Lou's lead. Mary Lou, run through it again and we'll take notes.

MARY LOU.   Uh ... uh ... I don't think I want to do that again ... I almost felt naked.

JO.   But it felt kinda good, didn't it? *(Rita plays that section of "REVOLUTIONARY ETUDE."*)*

MARY LOU.   STOP IT!

---

* See Special Note on Songs and Recordings on copyright page.

MICKEY.   I gotta admit — you sounded pretty good!

MO.   Excellent!

LEE.   It's going to work — it's actually going to work —

RITA.   Lee, you were the one who said it was going to work from the beginning —

LEE.   I know. But I didn't really believe it. It's never worked before.

MARY LOU.   You're the cowgirl, Jo.... There's no point in anybody singing tonight if you don't sing.

JO.   You're oversteppin' yourself. *(Mickey hands the envelope to Lee who opens and reads it.)*

MARY LOU.   I saw the pictures, Jo. And I saw the record offers.

JO.   You were up there snoopin' around!

MARY LOU.   It's where you belong.

JO.   You don't know what you're talkin' about.

MARY LOU.   I know I'm not singin' if you don't sing.

JO.   You're about as stubborn as a thirsty tick! *(To Lee.)* What's that letter?

LEE.   It's nothing. It's just a fax.

JO.   Well, hand it over.

LEE.   It's not for you. It's just a —

JO.   Course it's for me, nobody else gets faxes here! Hand it over.

LEE.   I'm sorry. It wasn't our business. I called my friend at the musician's union — we just thought if we found her —

RITA.   We didn't mean to butt in — we just thought — you know — Connie Carlson at the grand re-opening — would have been perfect ...

JO.   And all these years, I just thought she didn't want to come back. *(She reads from telegram.)* "Died August 13, 1963."

MO.   I'm sorry, Jo.

MICKEY.   I know you woulda liked to have seen her again.

MO.   Yeah.

JO.   Well, I guess I knew — she'd have been a big star if —

MARY LOU.   If nothin' — it's your turn. You've got no reason left not to sing.

JO.   I'm not singin'!!

MARY LOU.   You don't have to be scared. Just don't look down.

MO.   We gotta keep movin', Jo.

JO.   That's enough! I'm guessin' those costumes need pressin' and a few stitches. Be a shame if ya'll don't look as good as you're gonna sound. *(Beat.)* Go on — get out of here. I'm still the boss! *(Everyone exits.)*

    IT STARTS TO GET DARK, WE'RE ALL AT THE PARK

    THE GAME'S ALMOST THROUGH.

    I'M COVERED IN DIRT, BEN TORE HIS NEW SHIRT,

    MY KNEE'S BLACK AND BLUE.

    WE DON'T HAVE TO SAY IT'S BEEN SUCH A GREAT DAY,

    BUT WE JUST CAN'T PRETEND

    THAT ANYTIME NOW SOMEONE'S MOM WON'T ANNOUNCE

    IT'S TIME FOR OUR GOOD TIMES TO END.

    IT'S TIME TO COME HOME

    PICK UP YOUR GLOVE, DON'T FORGET YOUR HAT.

    SUPPER'S ON, DADDY'S HOME,

    WASH YOUR HANDS, HEY, IS THAT YOUR BAT?

    I IMAGINED THAT MOM HAD NOT REALLY GONE,

    THAT SHE WAS CALLIN' ME TOO.

    I'D GATHER MY STUFF AND TRY TO ACT TOUGH,

    BUT THE OTHER KIDS KNEW.

    THEY SAID I SHOULD BE GLAD THERE WAS NO ONE TO NAG ME

    TO COME HOME AT ALL.

    I COULD GO TO BED LATE, LEAVE THE PEAS ON MY PLATE,

    BUT I'D'VE DIED TO HAVE JUST HEARD HER CALL,

    JOSIE, TIME TO COME HOME.

    GIRL, YOUR FRECKLES LOOK JUST LIKE MINE.

I'D SAY, "MOM, DO YOU KNOW,

CAN I WEAR LIPSTICK WHEN I'M NINE?"

DID I LOOK LIKE SHE DID

WHEN SHE WAS A KID?

WOULD DAD LET HER SEE

PICTURES OF ME — If she asked.

BUT NOW I'M UP AND GROWN, I GOT KIDS OF MY OWN,

MAMA'S GONE NOW FOR GOOD.

I ALWAYS THOUGHT SHE WOULD TRY TO FIND ME,

AT LEAST I HOPED THAT SHE WOULD.

BUT WOULD I JUST HAVE SCREAMED, "WHERE WERE YOU IN MY TEENS?

WHERE WERE YOU WHEN I CRIED!"

THERE WAS SO MUCH TO SAY, BUT IF I SAW HER TODAY,

ALL I'D WANT TO SAY WOULD BE "GOOD-BYE."

SO IT'S TIME TO COME HOME.

KEEP YOUR CHIN UP, SHOW THEM YOU'RE STRONG.

TIME TO COME HOME,

GET ON STAGE BACK WHERE YOU BELONG.

ONE THING MAMA SAID,

"GIRL, IF I'M LIVIN' OR DEAD,

I'VE LEFT SOMETHING REAL,

NO ONE EVER CAN STEAL.

I'VE GIVEN YOU SONG —

JO, IT'S TIME TO COME HOME.

(Lights go to black. Lights up as Mickey and Mo enter carrying microphones.)

MO.   Testing. *(She blows in mike.)* Testing. Testing. Come on, Mic. Help me test the microphones.

MICKEY.   If I ain't singin' into a microphone, I ain't testin' a microphone.

(Mo goes to the second microphone. Mickey is setting up for the customers.)

MO.   Mickey. Mickey, can you hear me?

MICKEY.   Knock it off, Mo.

MO.   Come on, Mic. It's gonna be fun! Did you see there's already 127 people lined up outside? Bet you even break your chili carryin' record tonight, balance nine at once!

MICKEY.   Stop it, Mo. Don't you get it? This is the worst night of my life. There's gonna be girl singers on this stage for the first time in … in …

MO.   39 years.

MICKEY.   Right. And I'm gonna be slingin' chili.

MO.   I know. But it's just 'cause Jo needs ya so much on the floor. Everybody knows you're an excellent performer.

MICKEY.   Whatever.

MO.   Hey! Did you hear about the cow who jumped over the barbed-wire fence? It was an udder disaster! *(Pause.)* What do you get from a cow who has lost its memory?

MICKEY.   I don't know. What?

MO.   Milk of Amnesia!

MICKEY.   How come you ain't upset about not playin', Mo?

MO.   'Cause I get to run the cash register. I kinda like numbers pretty much, Mic.

MICKEY.   Do you really think I'm an excellent performer?

MO.   Superb.

MICKEY.   I got a knock-knock for ya.

MO.   OK.

MICKEY.   But you gotta start it.

MO.   OK. Knock-knock.

MICKEY.   Who's there?

MO.   *(After considerable thought.)* You're feelin' better, aren't ya?

MICKEY.   Come on, we gotta get ready to announce the show. *(Mickey exits.)*

MO.   Lights! *(Mo exits. On microphone, in darkness.)*

MICKEY.   Ladies and Gentlemen!

MO.   *(Echoing.)* Gentlemen, Gentlemen, Gentlemen.

MICKEY.   Thank you for coming to the grand reopening of Hiram Hall!

MO.   Hall, Hall, Hall.

MICKEY.   And now

MO.   Ow, ow, ow.

MICKEY.   it is my pleasure to introduce to you

MO.   the one —

MICKEY.   the only —

MO.   your friend and mine —

MICKEY and MO.   JO CARLSON! *(Lights up on Jo in full stage-costume cowgirl outfit.)*

JO.   Thank you, ladies and gentlemen, and welcome to Hiram Hall. I've wanted to say that for a long, long time. It's great to have so many old friends in the audience — folks I've spent a lot of good times with here — but tonight, it's not about lookin' back — it's about movin' on — and I am damn proud to introduce to ya'll the newest and most — interesting — act in country singin' anywhere — please welcome my favorite new all-girl group ... for the first time ever — The Cowgirl Trio. *(Mary Lou, Rita and Lee enter in full costume, riding Mo's cow, pulled by Mo.)*

TRIO.

> WE'RE A TRAVELLING TRIO AND WE DON'T COME FROM PARTS ROUND HERE.

> WE MADE A LUCKY DETOUR OFF THE HIGHWAY OF OUR CAREER.

RITA.

> TOOK A WRONG TURN AT THE LAST TOWN —

> THOUGHT WE WERE LOST, TROUBLE BOUND.

LEE.

> HAD A BREAKTHROUGH,

MARY LOU.

> HAD A BREAKDOWN,

TRIO.

> NOW IT SEEMS WE'RE FOUND.

> YOU CAN TAKE THOSE ROAD MAPS, THROW THEM AWAY,

> DON'T NEED DIRECTIONS

> OR TRIPLE A A-A-A-A-A

RITA.   Howdy, Rexford! It's a pleasure to be here. Thanks for havin' us! We're as pleased as a cow in a cabbage patch ... or something like that ... to be singin' for ya'll here in the sunflower state!

LEE.

THERE'S A SUNFLOWER OUT IN THE YARD

GROWING FROM SOIL DRY AND HARD

LEE and MARY LOU.

THOUGH I PASS BY IT EVERY DAY

DON'T NOTICE IT 'TIL TODAY.

TRIO.

SUNFLOWER, WITH YOUR YELLOW FACE,

SOMEHOW YOU SEEM OUT OF PLACE.

WITHOUT TENDING, YOU GREW TALL AND STRONG —

WHERE FOLKS THINK YOU DON'T BELONG.

(Bridge — instrumental.)

LEE.

THERE ARE SUNFLOWERS THAT TOUCH OUR LIVES.

IN A CRUEL WORLD THEY CONTINUE TO THRIVE —

LEE and MARY LOU.

LIKE THE SUNFLOWER AMONG THE WEEDS,

GROWING FROM SOME FORGOTTEN SEED.

TRIO.

SUNFLOWER SO BRAVE AND BRIGHT

SHINING THROUGH THE DARKEST NIGHT.

WITHOUT TENDING THEY GROW EVERYWHERE.

THOUGH THEY ARE COMMON, THEY'RE ALWAYS RARE.

(Mickey and Mo enter.)

LEE.

    THOU SHALT NOT WHINE IN THE KINGDOM OF

TRIO.

    COUNTRY.

JO.   Sing it, cowgirl!

LEE.

    FATHER GAMBLED 'WAY OUR SAVINGS,

    MOTHER HAD TO SELL HER HAIR.

    PREACHERS GAVE THE SAME OLD ANSWER:

    SOMETIMES LIFE DON'T TREAT YA FAIR.

    ALWAYS KNEW WAS SOMETHING BETTER,

    WOULD GET THERE THROUGH MY FAITH AND PRAYER.

    THEN I FOUND THE CHURCH OF REFUGE,

    COUNTRY MUSIC GOT ME THERE.

TRIO.

    THOU SHALT NOT WHINE IN THE KINGDOM OF COUNTRY.

    VENGEANCE IS MINE IN THE KINGDOM OF SONG.

    AND IF YOU GET THERE YOU'LL SURELY KNOW IT —

MICKEY and MO.

    DON'T BLOW IT!

TRIO.

    BLESSED ARE THE PICKERS!

MICKEY and MO.

    NOT THE CITY SLICKERS!

TRIO.

    IT'S THE PLACE WHERE WE BELONG!

LEE.   Take it, Mickey! *(Banjo break.)*

JO.   Miss Mickey!

LEE.

    SO NOW I AM A SINGER, NOT A MOTHER OR HOUSEWIFE

    AND BRINGING JOY TO OTHERS IS THE PURPOSE OF MY LIFE.

    THOUGH I HAVE CHANGED IN MANY WAYS, I SOMEHOW DON'T
        FEEL RIGHT

    IF I DON'T SEE THE OPRY EACH AND EVERY SATURDAY NIGHT

TRIO.

    EVERY SATURDAY NIGHT RIGHT AT FIVE TWENTY-TWO

    ON ROUTE 50 MY JOURNEY WOULD START.

    MY PENNIES AND NICKELS WERE TUCKED IN MY SHOE

    AND A NASHVILLE SONG TUCKED IN MY HEART.

LEE.   Take it, Rita! *(Piano break.)*

ALL BUT JO.

    OH, MY PENNIES AND NICKELS WERE TUCKED IN MY SHOE

    AND A NASHVILLE SONG TUCKED IN MY HEART.

JO.   Let's hear it for all the cowgirls! Ya'll are an inspiration. And with that in
mind, I think I'd like to sing a song myself. Follow me. E7. *(Mary Lou plays an
E7 on the guitar. The others will join in throughout.)*

    I SPOKE WHEN I WAS SPOKEN TO, WAS SEEN BUT NEVER HEARD.

    THEY DIDN'T SPARE THE ROD, AND WE READ THE HOLY WORD.

    DID WHAT DADDY TOLD ME WAS AFRAID TO QUESTION WHY,

    HE WAS MASTER OF THE HOUSE AND HE WOULD BE 'TIL HE DIED.

    MARRIED YOUNG AND INNOCENT TO SOMEONE JUST LIKE PA

    BUT DADDY DIDN'T LIKE HOW HE KEPT LAYIN' DOWN THE LAW.

    HE SAID, "NEVER LET SOME FELLA TELL YOU WHAT YOU CAN DO.

    IF I HADN'T TOLD YOUR MAMA SHE'D STILL BE HERE WITH YOU."

    HOUSE RULES — NOT TAKIN' ORDERS ANYMORE.

    HOUSE RULES — HERE'S YOUR HAT THERE'S THE DOOR.

    HOUSE RULES — MY NECK'S OUT OF THAT NOOSE.

    HOUSE RULES — I'M QUEEN OF THIS ROOST.

YOU TREAT ME GOOD, I'LL TREAT YOU FINE. I'LL BE YOUR DEVOTEE

THE BEST PART OF MY RULES IS THEY ALWAYS WORK BOTH WAYS.

DO UNTO OTHERS AND FORGIVE YOUR NEIGHBOR'S SINS.

YOU'LL GET YOUR CHIPS FOR NOTHIN' AND THE DEALER NEVER WINS.

NOW I THINK I'VE MADE IT CLEAR HOW THINGS ARE GONNA BE.

DON'T CALL BE DADDY'S GIRL OR SUGAR OR YOUR SWEET BABY.

I'M A WOMAN TO BE RECKONED WITH, THE CARDS BELONG TO ME.

DO I NEED TO SPELL IT OUT?

COMPANY.

R-E-S-P-E-C-T

HOUSE RULES — NO MORE MEEK AND MILD.

HOUSE RULES — EVERY CARD'S WILD.

HOUSE RULES — AM I FEELIN' FINE.

HOUSE RULES — THE PLACE IS FINALLY MINE.

HOUSE RULES — HEROES DON'T GO UNSUNG.

HOUSE RULES — THE GOOD DON'T DIE YOUNG.

HOUSE RULES — NICE GUYS FINISH FIRST.

HOUSE RULES — THERE AIN'T ANOTHER VERSE.

HOUSE RULES.

RITA. Let's hear it again for Jo Carlson!

LEE. And now, ladies and gentlemen … and Jo, we got a little surprise for you. (*The trio takes their seated "classical" positions only to break into country after the first few bars.*)

DON'T HAVE TO BE DALE EVANS OR CALAMITY JANE.

DON'T HAVE TO WEAR BUCKSKIN AND SING LIKE DORIS DAY.

WE DON'T WEAR BIG WIGS, OR STRING TIES OR SPANGLY CLOTHES

OR SING SONGS ANYBODY KNOWS.

(Chorus.)

    BUT WE'RE COWGIRLS,

    WE'RE THE SPIRIT OF THIS LAND.

    WE'RE FREE TO BE

    A COUNTRY CLASSICAL BAND.

(Classical break.)

MARY LOU.

    I USED TO PLAY THE VIOLIN, NOW I FIDDLE AWAY.

(Break.)

LEE.

    WE ONLY PLAYED THE CLASSICS UP 'TIL YESTERDAY.

(Break.)

RITA.

    WE NEVER MILKED COWS

LEE.

    OR RODE BULLS

MARY LOU.

    OR BIRTHED A CALF

TRIO.

    OR CALLED A MAN MY BETTER HALF.

(Chorus. Instrumental.)

LEE.   What's that comin' down the tracks?

RITA.   Sounds like the Hiram Special! *(Instrumental. Yodel section. Final instrumental.)* and 1, 2 — 1, 2, 3, 4!

ENTIRE COMPANY.

    BUT WE'RE COWGIRLS, WE'RE THE SPIRIT OF THIS LAND.

    WE'RE FREE TO BE A COUNTRY CLASSICAL (COUNTRY CLASSICAL, COUNTRY CLASSICAL).

    BAND!

    YEE-HAW!!

PROPERTY LIST

Violin (MARY LOU)
Cello (LEE)
Piano (RITA)
Brochure (RITA)
Supplies (MO)
Auto harp (MO)
Banjo (MICKEY)
Ukulele (MO)
Coffee cup (MO)
Old box of photos (MO)
Mandolin (JO, MARY LOU)
Guitars (JO, LEE, MARY LOU)
Song sheets (RITA)
Picture frames with photographs (JO)
Bucket and brushes (MO, RITA)
Cowgirl hat (MO)
Life-size cow, on rope (MO)
Papers with financial statements (MO)
Outside decorations (MO, MICKEY)
Order pad (MICKEY)
Envelope with paper (MICKEY)
Microphones (MICKEY, JO)

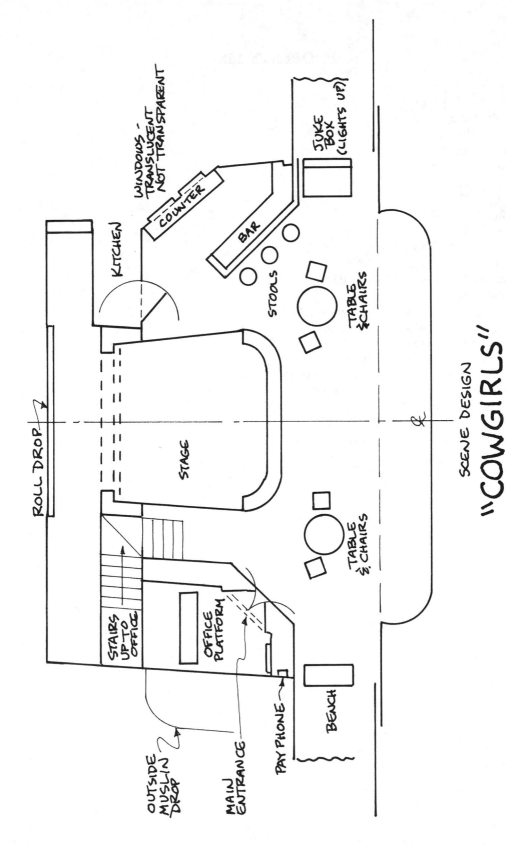

SCENE DESIGN

"COWGIRLS"

(DESIGNED BY JAMES NOONE FOR THE OLD GLOBE THEATRE)